2ND EDITION

LEVEL **3B**

PIANO
Adventures®
by Nancy and Randall Faber

THE BASIC PIANO METHOD

T0004698

Student's Name: _____

Production: Jon Ophoff
Cover and Illustrations: Terpstra Design, San Francisco
Engraving: Dovetree Productions, Inc.

ISBN 978-1-61677-180-5

Progress Chart

Keep track of your progress.
Color or put a star sticker for each item.

		Lesson	Theory	Technique	Performance	Sightreading
☆	Get Ready for Take-off! (Level 3A Review)	4-5				

UNIT 1 Key of A Minor

		Lesson	Theory	Technique	Performance	Sightreading
☆	A Natural Minor Scale, A Harmonic Minor Scale	6		2, 4		
☆	Primary Chords: i, iv, V7, Two-Octave A Minor Scales	7	2	2, 5		
☆	Energico (*sfz*)	8-9	3	6		6-9
☆	Fiesta España (motive and sequence)	10-11	4-5		2-3	10-13
☆	Snowfall	12-13		3, 7, 8-9		

UNIT 2 Key of E Minor

		Lesson	Theory	Technique	Performance	Sightreading
☆	E Natural Minor Scale, E Harmonic Minor Scale	14		10		
☆	Primary Chords: i, iv, V7, Two-Octave E Minor Scales	15	6	11		
☆	Sea Chantey (theme and variation, cut time review)	16-17	7	12-13	4-6	14-19
☆	Rage Over a Lost Penny (Beethoven) (ternary form review)	18-19	8		7	20-23
☆	Playing a Lead Sheet: *Finale* (Dvořák)	20-21	9			24-27

UNIT 3 Key of D Minor

		Lesson	Theory	Technique	Performance	Sightreading
☆	D Natural Minor Scale, D Harmonic Minor Scale	22				
☆	Primary Chords: i, iv, V7, Two-Octave D Minor Scales	23	10	14-15		
☆	Cat Patrol (articulation)	24-25	11	16-17	8-9	
☆	Baroque Dance (Speer)	26				28-31
☆	Legend of Madrid (grace note, cadenza)	27-29	12-13	18-19	10-11	32-35

FF118

Get Ready for Take-off!
(Level 3A Review)

- Define $\frac{6}{8}$ for your teacher.
  Now play this rhythm on an **F major chord**. Count aloud.

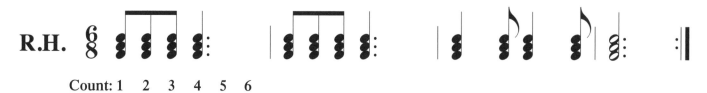

Count: 1 2 3 4 5 6

- Define $\frac{4}{4}$ for your teacher.
  Now play this rhythm on a **D major chord**. Count aloud.

Count: 1 + a 2 + a 3 + a 4 + a

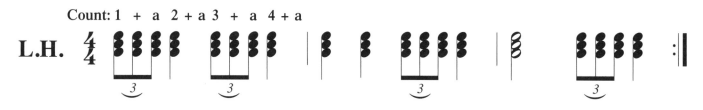

- Fill in the blanks below.

  Ritardando means _____

  The term *a tempo* means _____

  ₵ means ___ counts in a measure. The ___ receives 1 count.

Reading

- Name each interval in the blank: **2nd**, **3rd**, **4th**, **5th**, **6th**, **7th**
  Now play each on the keyboard.

- Write these **ledger line** notes:

upper ledger lines
A   C   E

lower ledger lines
A   C   E

Theory

- Write the correct letter names.

Key of G
tonic note _____

Key of F
dominant note _____

Key of D
leading tone _____

- Add the correct **sharps** or **flats** in front of the notes for each scale.

G major scale

F major scale

D major scale

Chromatic scale passage

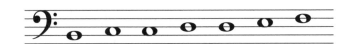

- Label these examples as **I**, **IV**, or **V7** chords.

Key of G

_____

Key of D

_____

Key of F

_____

Key of C

_____

Symbols and Terms

- Write these **dynamic marks** in order from softest to loudest.

f *ff* *mp* *mf* *p* *pp*

softest   loudest

- Fill in the blanks below. Then play a **D major scale** at each tempo mark.

Andante means _____

Allegro means _____

Moderato means _____

Vivace means _____

- Under each note draw:

a *staccato* mark

an accent mark

a *tenuto* (stress) mark

Key of A Minor

Every major key has a minor key that shares the *same* key signature.
This minor key is called the RELATIVE MINOR.

The relative minor starts on the **6th tone of the major scale**.
You can also count **3 half steps down** from the tonic of the major key.

The key of A minor is the relative minor of C major.

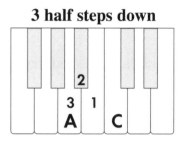

1. Play each scale and *listen* to the sound.

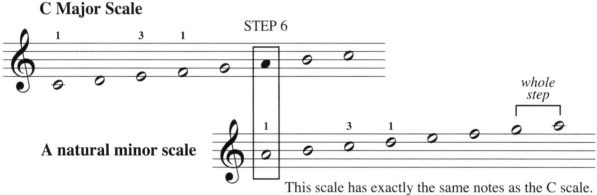

This scale has exactly the same notes as the C scale.

A Natural Minor Scale

2. Practice hands separately, then hands together.

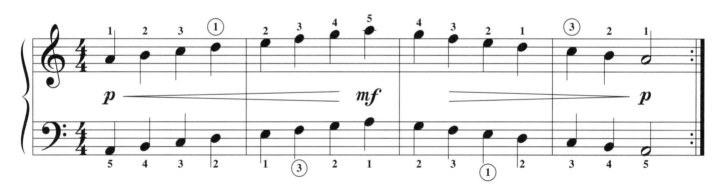

For the harmonic minor scale, raise the 7th tone a half step.
This creates a half step between scale degrees 7 and 8 — the *leading tone* to the *tonic*.

A Harmonic Minor Scale

3. Practice hands separately, then hands together.

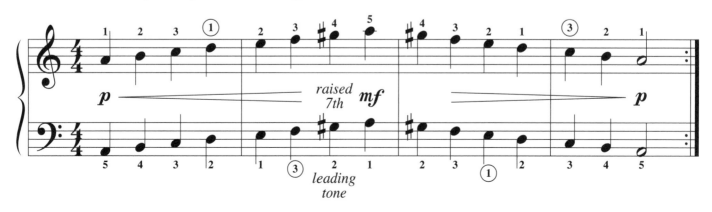

Primary Chords in A Minor: i iv V7

4. Practice hands separately, then hands together.
In a minor key, the **i** and **iv** chords are minor and shown in **lower case Roman numerals**.

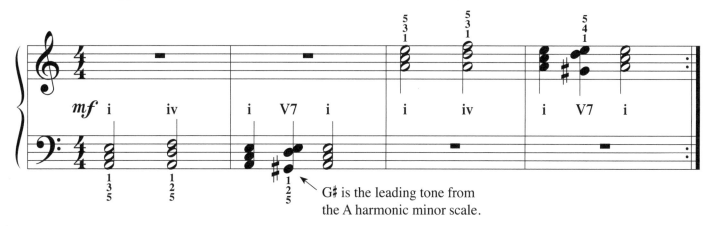

G♯ is the leading tone from
the A harmonic minor scale.

5. Now play this L.H. Alberti bass pattern.

Roman numerals: i   iv   i   V7   i

Challenge: Two-Octave A Minor Scales*

6. Practice these scales s-l-o-w-l-y.

- First play *without* the G♯ to form the **A natural minor scale**.

- Repeat *with* the G♯ to form the **A harmonic minor scale**.

*Teacher Note: The melodic minor scale is
introduced in the Level 5 Lesson Book.

F1180   ✏️Theory p.2   ✋Tech p.2 (The Up-Touch), p.5   7

sfz – *sforzando*   A sudden, strong accent on a single note or chord.

- Which form of the A minor scale is used in this piece?
  natural or **harmonic**

- Which two primary chords are used in *measures 1-16*?
  i   **iv** or **V7**

Energico*

Key of A Minor

N. Faber

Energico is Italian for energetic, vigorous, or powerful.

🖉 Theory p.3   ✎ Tech p.6   ᔐ Sight pp.6-9

F1180

9

Motive and Sequence

motive—a short musical pattern.

sequence—a musical pattern repeated on another pitch.
A sequence may be higher or lower than the motive.

- This motive uses *syncopation*—notes accented
  BETWEEN the beats.

Fiesta España

Key of A Minor

N. Faber

✏ Theory pp.4-5   🎵 Perf pp.2-3   👓 Sight pp.10-13

FF118

DISCOVERY Name the four **chords** used in this piece: ___ minor ___ major ___ major ___ major

Often a piece in a major key goes to the **relative minor** for harmonic variety, then returns to the major.

- In what measure does *Snowfall* go to the relative minor?

- First learn the R.H. melody. Notice the fingering.

- Then play hands together. Keep the L.H. thumb *very* soft—as light as a snowflake!

Snowfall

Key of ____ **Major / Minor** (circle)

Gently moving (♩ = 100-112)

N. Faber

Shape the phrase with the crescendo and diminuendo.

Tech p.3 (Voicing the Melody), p.7, pp.8-9

FF118C

Key of E Minor

The key of E minor is the RELATIVE MINOR of G major.
E minor and **G major** share the same key signature: 1 sharp.

Review: Think 3 half steps down from the tonic of the major key.

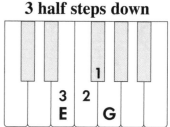

1. Play each scale and *listen* to the sound.

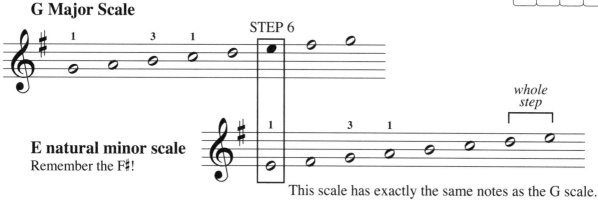

G Major Scale

E natural minor scale
Remember the F♯!

STEP 6

whole step

This scale has exactly the same notes as the G scale.

E Natural Minor Scale

2. Practice hands separately, then hands together.

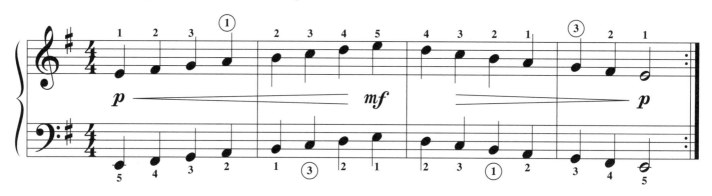

Remember, for the harmonic minor scale, raise the 7th tone a half step.
This creates a half step between scale degrees 7 and 8—the *leading tone* to the *tonic*.

E Harmonic Minor Scale

3. Practice hands separately, then hands together.

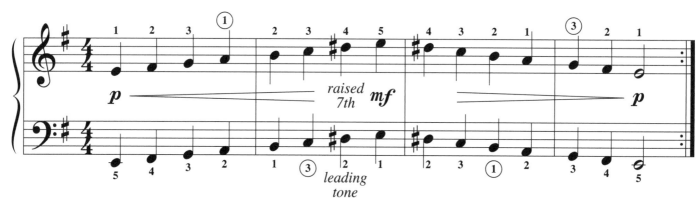

raised 7th

leading tone

Primary Chords in E Minor: i iv V7

4. Practice hands separately, then hands together.
Remember, in a minor key, the **i** and **iv** chords are minor.

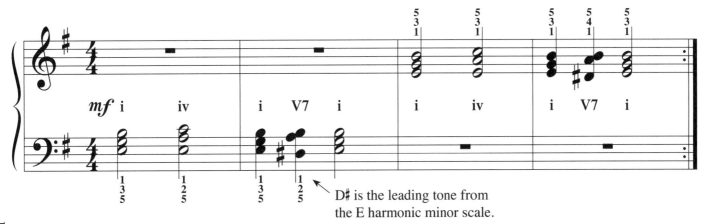

D♯ is the leading tone from
the E harmonic minor scale.

5. Now play this L.H. Alberti bass pattern.

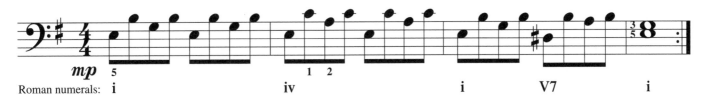

Roman numerals: i   iv   i   V7   i

Challenge: Two-Octave E Minor Scales

6. Practice these scales s-l-o-w-l-y.

- First play *without* the D♯ to form the **E natural minor scale**.

- Repeat *with* the D♯ to form the **E harmonic minor scale**.

Cut Time Review

$\mathbf{C} = \frac{2}{2}$ beats in a measure

the ♩ gets one beat

Cut time is notated the same as $\frac{4}{4}$ time,
but is played feeling **2 beats per measure**.

Sea Chantey*

Key of _____ **Major/Minor**

Theme
With energy (♩ = 92-100)

Traditional melody
arranged

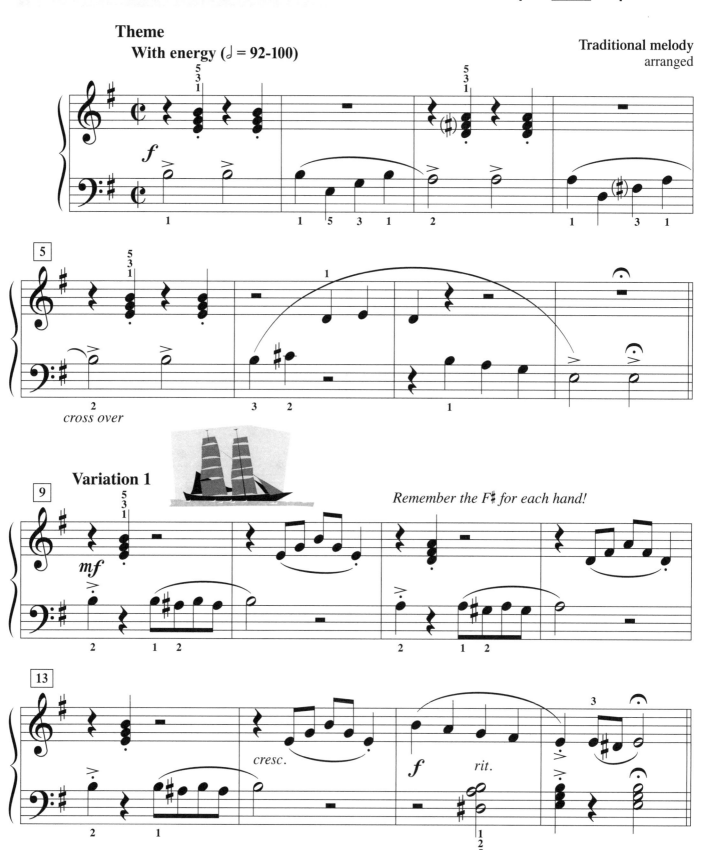

cross over

Variation 1

Remember the F♯ for each hand!

cresc.

rit.

*A chantey is an energetic sailor song.

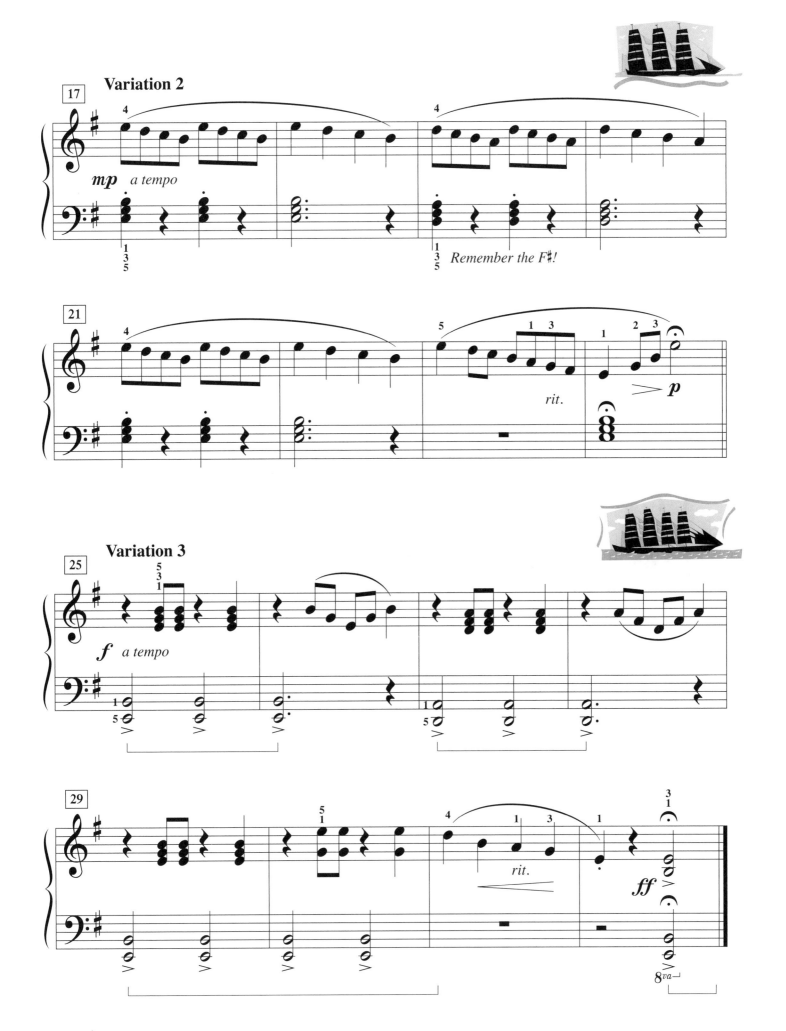

C R E A T I V E Can you make up your own **variation** of *Sea Chantey*?
(Hint: Change the rhythm, notes, dynamics, etc.)

Beethoven wrote some of the world's greatest music but also had a humorous side as seen in this composition.

Another famous composer, Robert Schumann, wrote of the piece, "It would be difficult to find anything merrier than this whim... It is the most amiable, harmless anger, similar to that felt when one cannot pull a shoe from off the foot."

Enjoy this entertaining classical piece!

- First practice the R.H. alone. Notice the fingering.

- Listen for crisp *staccatos* as you play hands together.

Rage Over a Lost Penny*

Key of _____ Major/Minor

Ludwig van Beethoven
(1770–1827, Germany)
arranged

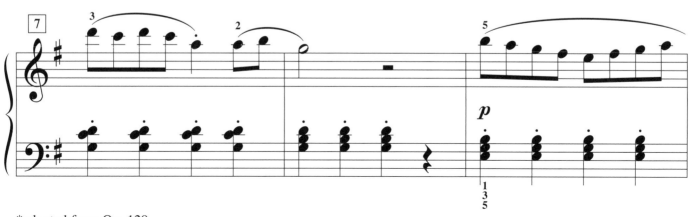

*adapted from Op. 129

Theory p.8   Perf p.7   Sight pp.20-23

DISCOVERY This piece is in **A B A** form (also called ternary form).
Label the **A** section, **B** section, and **A** section in your music.

Playing a Lead Sheet

Review: A *lead sheet* consists of a melody with **chord symbols** shown above the staff. The chord symbols indicate the harmony to be played with your left hand.

Directions for Finale

- First play the melody alone on page 21.

- Next play the blocked chord warm-up below.

- Now play the melody with **blocked chords** as shown by the chord symbols.

Blocked Chord Warm-up

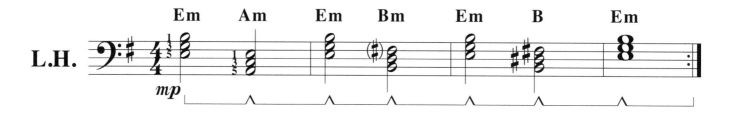

- Now practice this broken chord warm-up.

- Challenge: Play the melody slowly with this L.H. accompaniment. See the example below.

Broken Chord Warm-up

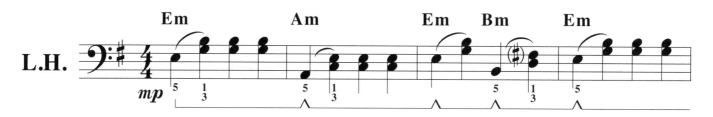

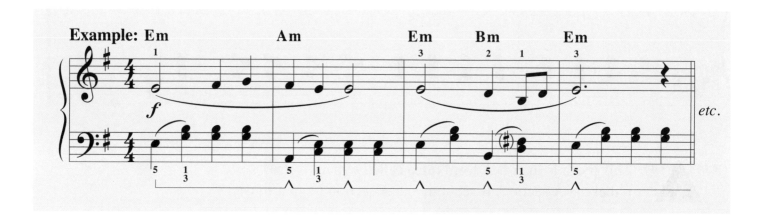

20

Finale

from Symphony No. 9, "From the New World"

Key of _____ **Major/Minor**

Antonín Dvořák
(1841–1904, Czech)

Key of D Minor

The key of D minor is the RELATIVE MINOR of F major.
D minor and **F major** share the same key signature: 1 flat.

Review: Think 3 half steps down from the tonic of the major key.

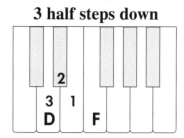

3 half steps down

1. Play each scale and *listen* to the sound.

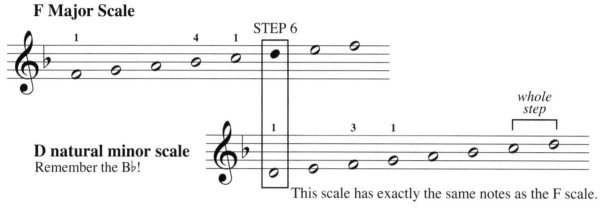

F Major Scale

STEP 6

D natural minor scale
Remember the B♭!

This scale has exactly the same notes as the F scale.

D Natural Minor Scale

2. Practice hands separately, then hands together.

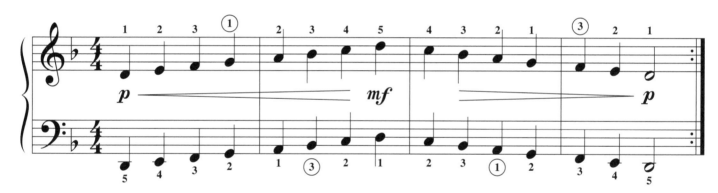

Remember, for the harmonic minor scale, raise the 7th tone a half step.
This creates a half step between scale degrees 7 and 8—the *leading tone* to the *tonic*.

D Harmonic Minor Scale

3. Practice hands separately, then hands together.

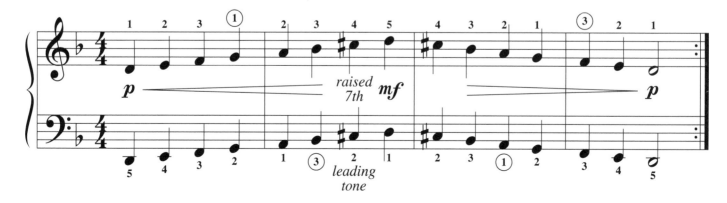

FF1180

Primary Chords in D Minor: i   iv   V7

4. Practice hands separately, then hands together.
In a minor key, the **i** and **iv** chords are minor.

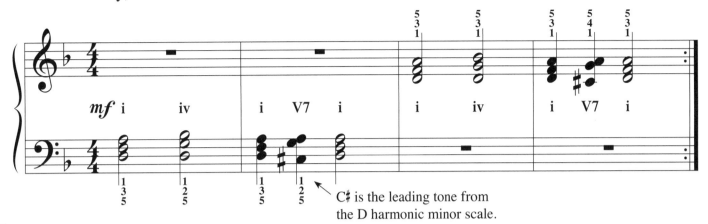

C♯ is the leading tone from the D harmonic minor scale.

5. Now play this L.H. Alberti bass pattern.

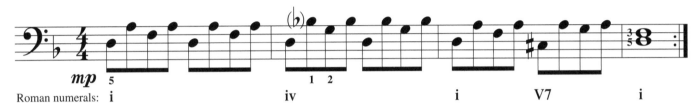

Roman numerals: i   iv   i   V7   i

Challenge: Two-Octave D Minor Scales

6. Practice these scales s-l-o-w-l-y.

• First play *without* the C♯ to form the **D natural minor scale**.

• Repeat *with* the C♯ to form the **D harmonic minor scale**.

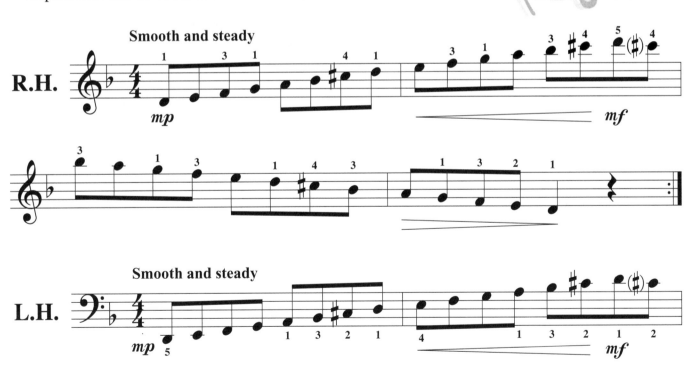

Smooth and steady

R.H.

Smooth and steady

L.H.

Articulation refers to the different kinds of touch used to play the keyboard—*legato*, *staccato*, accent, and *tenuto*.

• Capture the mysterious, yet playful character of *Cat Patrol* by carefully observing the articulations for each hand.

Cat Patrol

Key of _____ Major/Minor

N. Faber

🖊Theory p.11   ✎Tech pp.16-17   ✂Perf pp.8-9   FF118

Baroque Dance

Key of ____ Major/Minor

- Label the **A** and **B sections** of this binary form piece.

Daniel Speer
(1636–1707, Germany)
original form

Allegretto (♩ = 100-116)

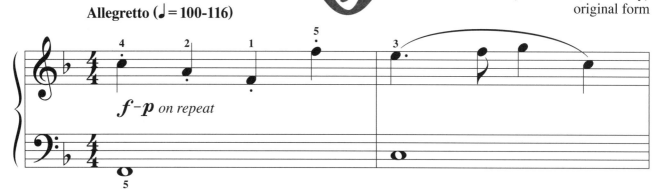

f-*p* on repeat

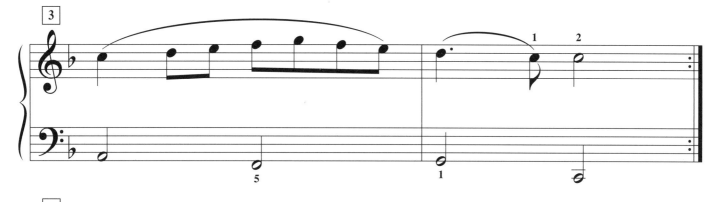

mf-*p* on repeat

Your teacher may demonstrate the optional trill (*tr*).

cresc. (on repeat)

f

DISCOVERY Does the L.H. in the **A section** end on the *tonic* or *dominant* note?

FF118

Grace note

A small note with a slash. It is an ornamental note, played quickly into the note that follows.
(See page 28. Your teacher will demonstrate.)

Legend of Madrid

Key of _____ Major/Minor

N. Faber

With motion, "in two" (♩. = 69-84)

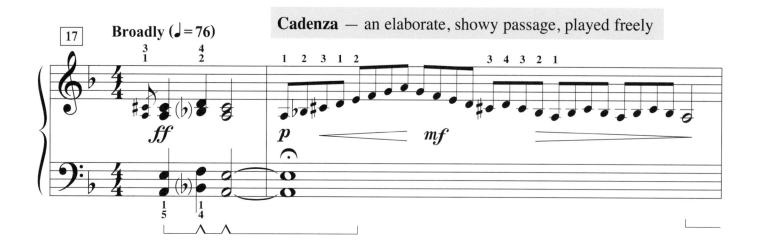

Cadenza — an elaborate, showy passage, played freely

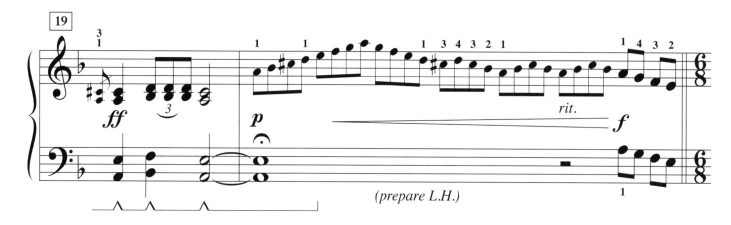

(prepare L.H.)

With motion, "in two"

DISCOVERY The form of this piece is **A B A coda**. Find and label each section in your music.

Interval Review

R.H.

2nd   3rd   4th   5th   6th   7th   8ve
(octave)

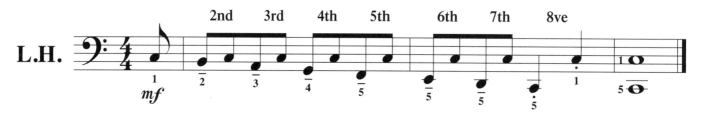

L.H.

2nd   3rd   4th   5th   6th   7th   8ve

• Transpose each hand to **G major** and **D major**.
(Remember the sharps!)

Octave Playing

• Play this C major scale in **octaves**. Spring *lightly* from the keys as you play each octave.

• Prepare the next octave during the rest.

Note: Omit this exercise if the student cannot reach an octave.

The Scale in Octaves

Steady (♩ = 108-120)

relax   relax   relax   relax

f-p

Repeat p

CREATIVE
Explore playing *Twinkle, Twinkle Little Star* with **R.H. octaves** in the key of G major. Play by ear, beginning on a G octave. Repeat with **L.H. octaves**.

Leopold Mozart was the father of the famous composer Wolfgang Amadeus Mozart.

Form Check: This minuet is in two parts (A B form). Is two-part form called **binary form** or **ternary form?** _____

Minuet in F

Leopold Mozart
(1719–1787, Germany)
original form

DISCOVERY

Does the L.H. in the **B section** begin on the *tonic* or *dominant* note?

Grace Note Warm-up

- Practice these examples.
  (Your teacher will demonstrate.)

Phantom of the Keys

Key of _____ Major/Minor

Mischievous, with energy (♩=88-100)

N. Faber

🖉 Theory pp.14-15   ✋Tech p.21   👓Sight pp.36-39

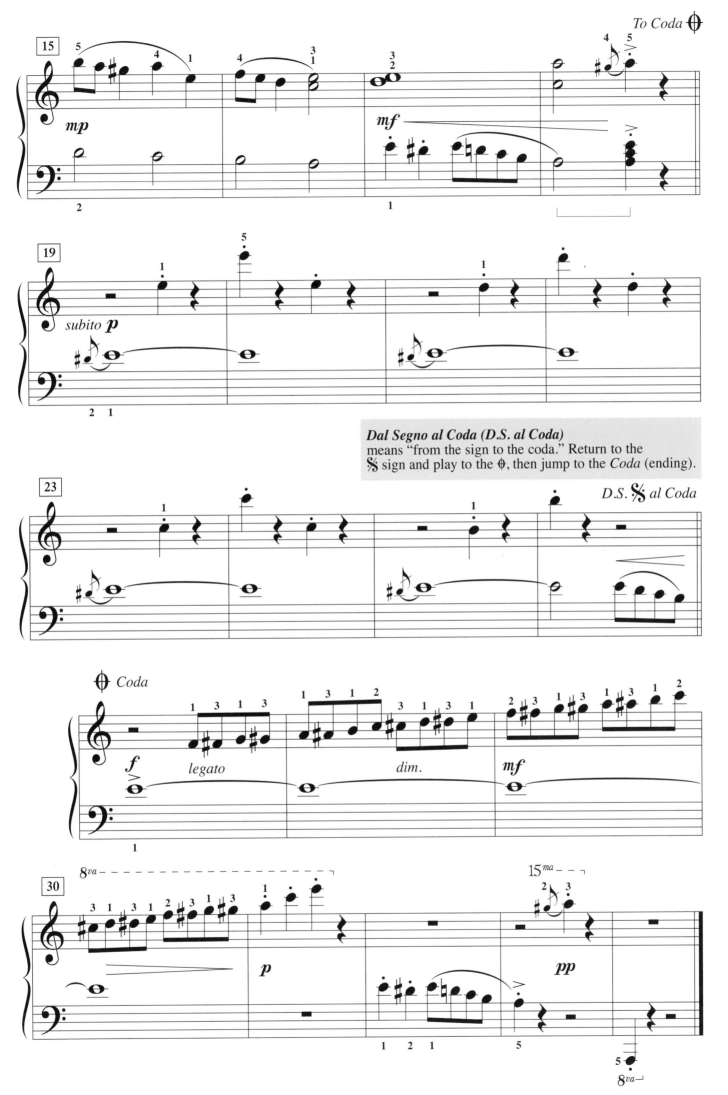

A *humoresque* is an instrumental piece of humorous quality.

Ostinato Review

An *ostinato* is a musical pattern repeated over and over.

• Name the two intervals used for this L.H. ostinato.

_____ and _____

Humoresque

Key of _____ Major/Minor

N. Faber

With mischief (♩ = 84-96)

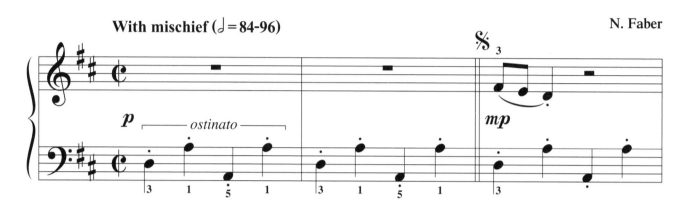

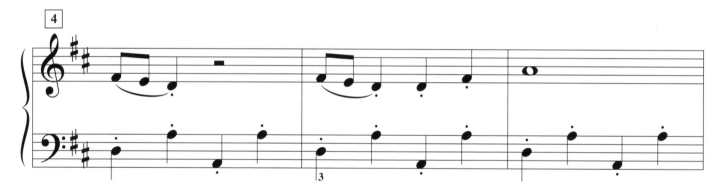

Perf pp.12-13   Sight pp.40-45

FF118

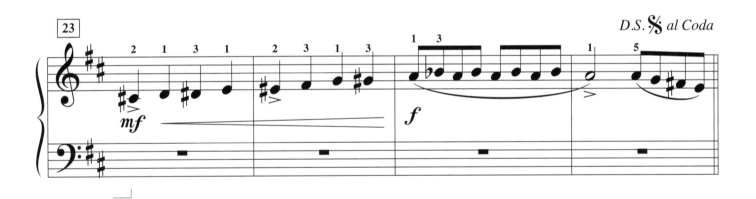

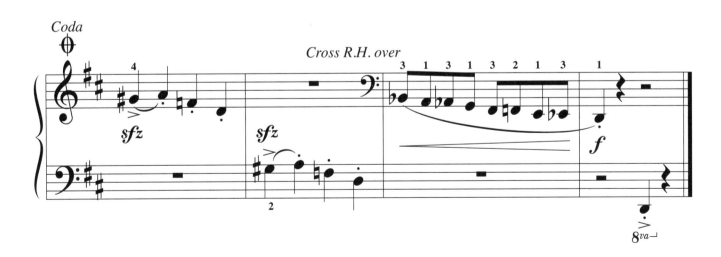

DISCOVERY In what measure does the music change from **D major** to **D minor**?

- The L.H. uses only one interval. What is it? _____

- What is the musical term for a repeating pattern? _____

- The R.H. uses only two intervals. Name them. _____ and _____

- There is no key signature but there is a "tonal center." What is it? _____

The Bear

Vladimir Rebikov
(1866–1920, Russia)
original form

- Play the **R.H. alone**. Notice the articulations—
  staccatos and *tenutos*. Are there any slurs?

- Play **hands together** slowly.
  Bring out all the dynamics.

Andante (♩ = 88-100)

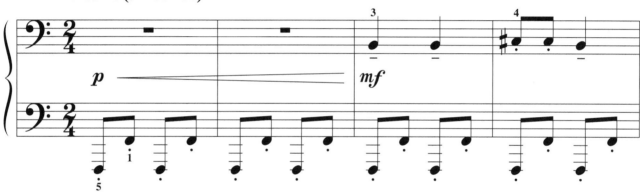

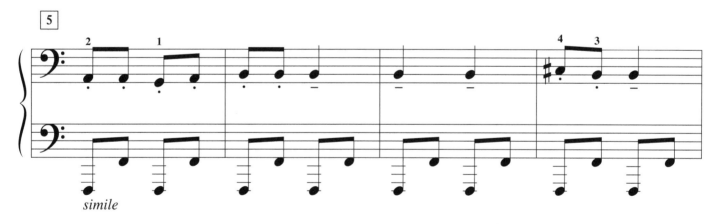

simile

🖉Theory pp.16-17   ✎Tech pp.22-23   ♪Perf pp.14-15   ✍Sight pp.46-49

DISCOVERY Identify and explain these terms for your teacher:

andante (measure 1)   *tenuto* (measure 3)   *simile* (measure 5)

Intervals: Major and Minor 3rds

Major 3rd — abbreviated **M3**
The major 3rd spans 2 whole steps or 4 half steps.

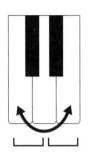 

melodic M3   harmonic M3

1. Find and play these **Major 3rds**.

D, up a major 3rd to _____?

F, up a major 3rd to _____?

minor 3rd — abbreviated **m3**
The minor 3rd spans a whole step plus a half step, or 3 half steps.

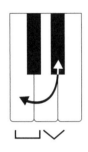 

melodic m3   harmonic m3

2. Find and play these **minor 3rds**.

G, up a minor 3rd to _____?

E, up a minor 3rd to _____?

Major and Minor Triads

A triad is a 3-note chord built in 3rds.
The 3 notes of a triad are the **root**, **3rd**, and **5th**.

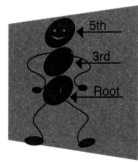

8 5th
3rd
root

F Major triad

— Major 3rd

F minor triad

— minor 3rd

3. • Play the **root** and **3rd** of the F major triad.
Listen to the sound of the major 3rd.

• Now play the triad.
Listen to the sound of the **major triad**.

4. • Play the **root** and **3rd** of the F minor triad.
Listen to the sound of the minor 3rd.

• Now play the triad.
Listen to the sound of the **minor triad**.

The 12 Major and Minor Triads

• Practice this triad exercise going up the keyboard **chromatically** (by half steps).

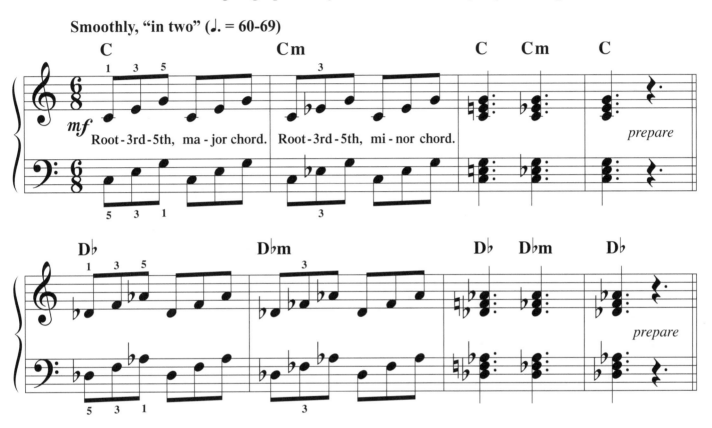

• Use the chart below to continue, beginning on **D**, **E♭**, **E**, **F**, **F♯**, **G**, **A♭**, **A**, **B♭**, **B**, and **C**.

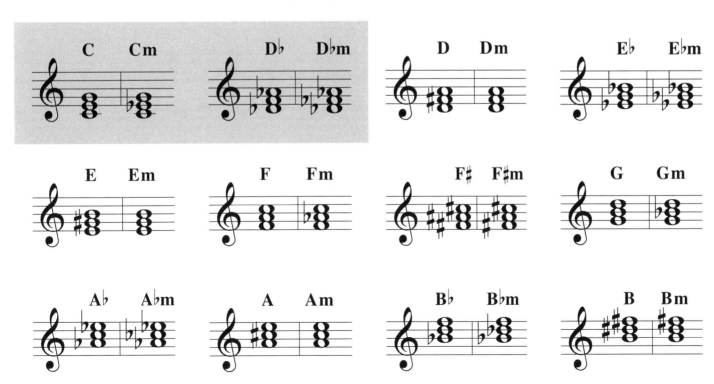

Triad Quiz

- Write the name for each triad below.
  Use a **capital letter** for *major*. Ex: G
  Use a capital letter with a **small m** for *minor*. Ex: Gm

Ex: <u>F#</u> ____ ____ ____ ____ ____ ____

- Now play each triad on the piano.

Tropical Island

Lazy and relaxed (♩ = 80-88)

N. Faber

Remember the F#!

CREATIVE Create an extended ending by playing the F# and G major chords going down the keyboard. End with the final *pianissimo* chord.

New Time Signature

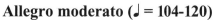

$\frac{6}{4}$ = 6 beats in a measure
the ♩ gets the beat

Think of $\frac{6}{4}$ as a combination of $\frac{3}{4} + \frac{3}{4}$:
♩ ♩ ♩ + ♩ ♩ ♩

Franz Liszt

Liebestraum
(Dream of Love, No. 3)

Key of _____ Major/Minor

Franz Liszt
(1811–1886, Hungary)
arranged

Allegro moderato (♩ = 104-120)

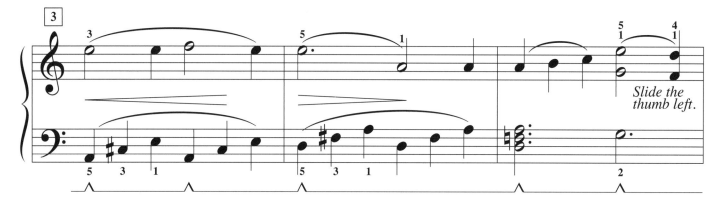

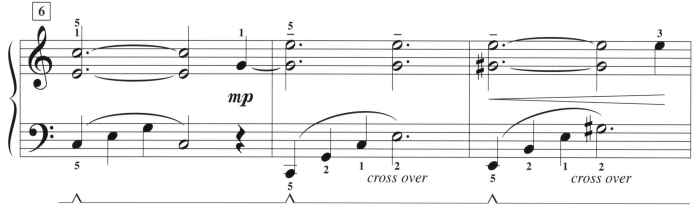

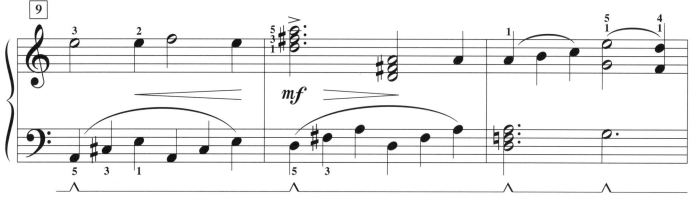

Arpeggiated or Rolled Chord: The wavy line indicates to play the notes quickly, bottom to top.

Exploring the 12-Bar Blues

The blues often uses three chords built on steps **1**, **4**, and **5** of the major scale.
The Roman numerals **I**, **IV**, and **V** are used to name these chords.

1. Play and say, **"I chord,"** **"IV chord,"** and **"V chord."**

Blues Facts

The word *bar* means measure. The 12-bar blues is a repeating pattern of chords—a **chord progression**.

It can be played with only three chords: **I**, **IV**, and **V**.

The Key of C Blues

2.
  • Practice and memorize this 12-bar blues progression.
  • Then play hands together with the R.H. one octave higher.

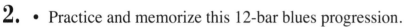

Count aloud: I 2 - 3 - 4   I 2 - 3 - 4   I 2 - 3 - 4   I 2 - 3 - 4

IV 2 - 3 - 4   IV 2 - 3 - 4   I 2 - 3 - 4   I 2 - 3 - 4

V 2 - 3 - 4   IV 2 - 3 - 4   I 2 - 3 - 4   I 2 - 3 - 4

D I S C O V E R Y Can you learn the Teacher Duet?

Teacher Duet: (Student plays *as written.*)

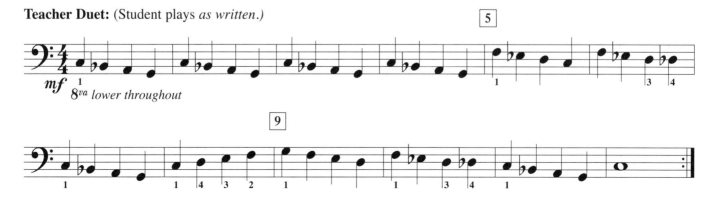

mf 8*va lower throughout*

FF11

Swing Rhythm Review

Remember, in **swing rhythm**, 8th notes are played in a *long-short* pattern.

Tap:

l-o-n-g   short   l-o-n-g   short   l-o-n-g   short   l-o-n-g

In the early 1900s, blues pianists sometimes performed in shacks called barrelhouses. The barrelhouse piano style has a steady, repeating **left-hand pattern**.

- First practice the **L.H.** alone for smooth hand position changes.

- Then practice slowly **hands together**. *Listen* for a steady beat!

Barrelhouse Blues

Moderately slow (♩ = 96-104)

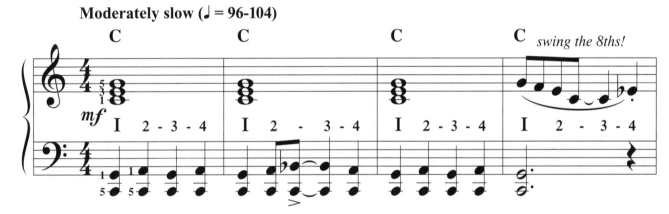

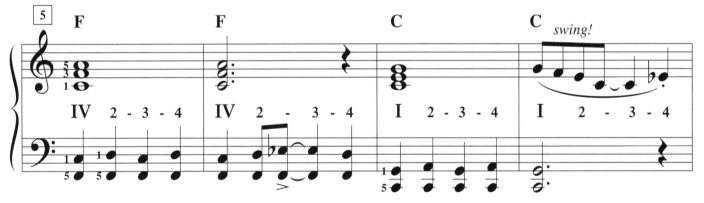

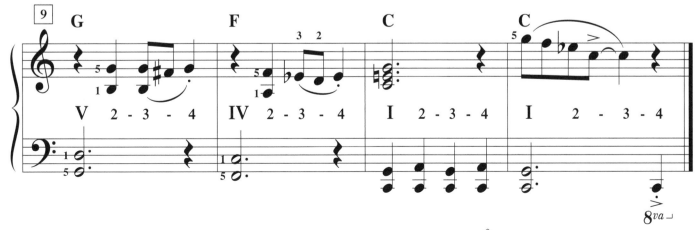

Walking Bass Pattern

This 12-bar blues piece features a "walking bass" pattern based on major and minor triads.

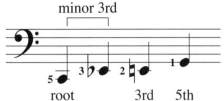

The Piano Playin' Chocolate Eater's Blues

Lyrics by Jennifer MacLean
Music by N. Faber

Chord Inversions: Three Positions for Triads

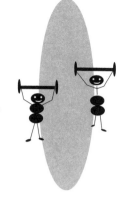

The notes of a triad can be rearranged, or *inverted*. The letter names stay the same. Every triad has 3 positions: **root position**, **1st inversion**, and **2nd inversion**.

• Play these 3 positions for the C major triad. *Listen* to the sound!

Root Position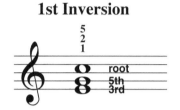

The **root** is the lowest note.

1st Inversion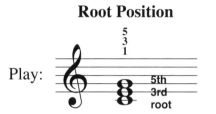

The **3rd** is the lowest note.

2nd Inversion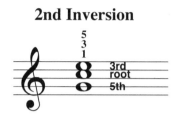

The **5th** is the lowest note.

> The chord name (root) is the *upper note* of the interval of a **4th**.

• Watch as your teacher demonstrates.

• Your turn! Play slowly and memorize.

1. C Major Chord Inversions

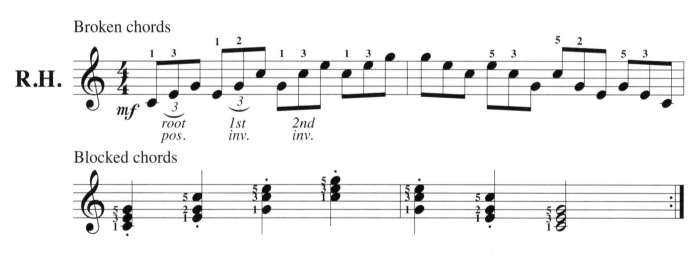

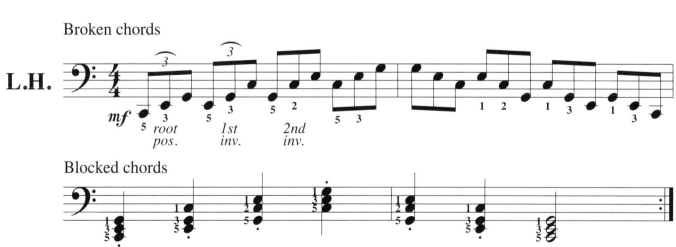

FF118

2. G Major Chord Inversions

R.H.

L.H.

- Transpose to **A minor**, **D minor**, and **F major**.

- Write the **chord letter names** in the boxes. Remember the chord root is the *upper note* of the 4th.

Inversion Etude

Andante (♩ = 80)

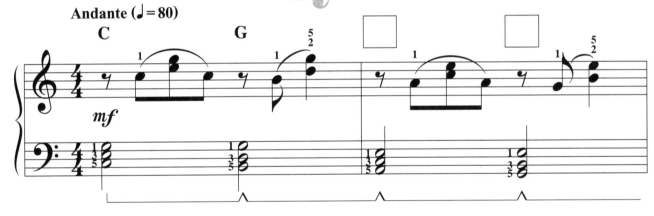

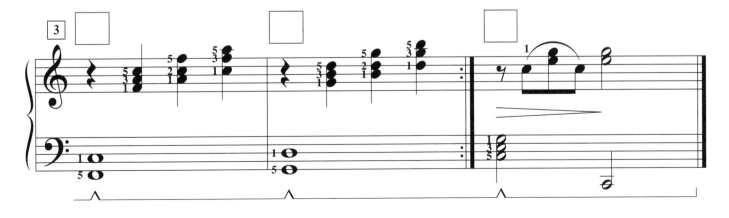

Theory p.22   49

A gavotte is a dance in moderate 4/4 time, popularized in 18th century France.

Rounded Binary Form

When part of the A section returns *within* the B section, the form is **rounded binary**.

• Is *Gavotte* in binary form or rounded binary form?

Gavotte

Benjamin Carr
(1768–1831, U.S.A.)
original form

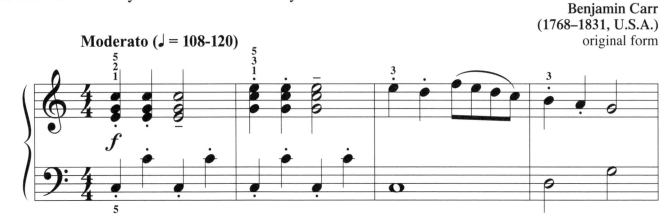

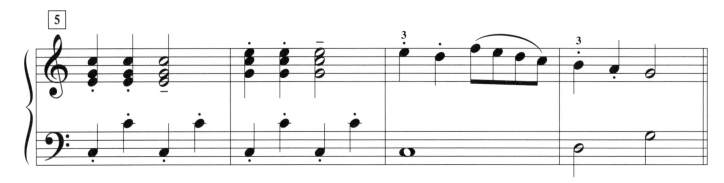

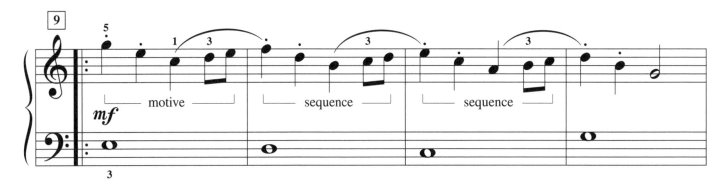

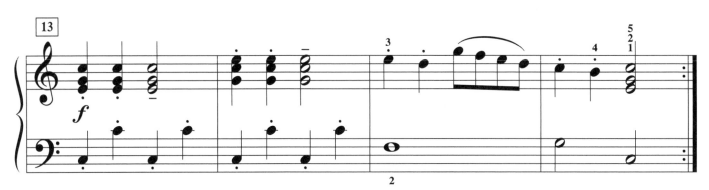

DISCOVERY

Can you play *Gavotte* by **memory**?

🖉 Theory p.23   🎵 Tech p.30   🎼 Sight pp.64-67   FF11

- First play slowly feeling **6 beats** per measure.

- When ready, play *vivace* feeling **2 beats** per measure.

The Return

Cornelius Gurlitt
(1820–1901, Germany)
original form

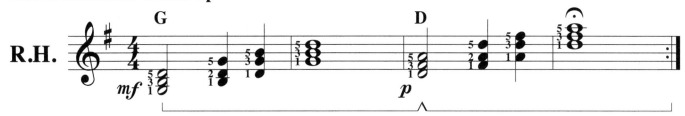

Swing Low, Sweet Chariot

Key of _____ Major/Minor

Moderately slow, with swing (♩ = 69-76)

Spiritual
arranged

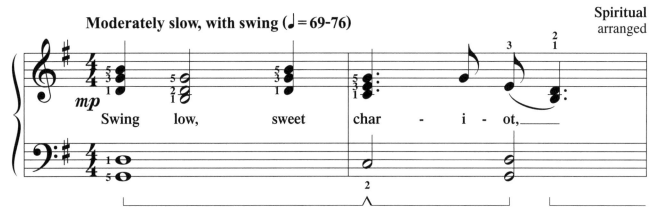

Swing   low,   sweet   char - i - ot,____

swing the 8ths!

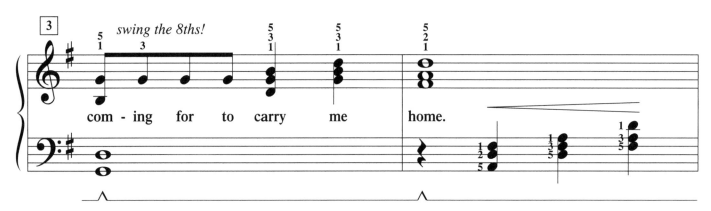

com - ing   for   to   carry   me   home.

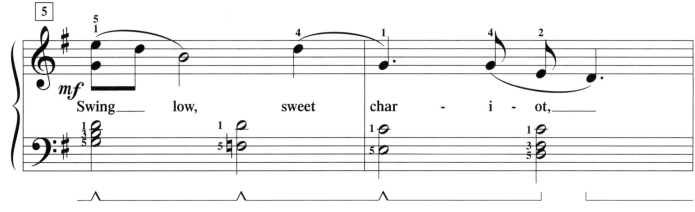

Swing____   low,   sweet   char - i - ot,____

Sixteenth (16th) Notes

2 flags — sixteenth note   2 flags — sixteenth rest

Four 16th notes = one quarter note

2 beams →

Count: **1** e + a   **1**

Feeling the Rhythm

- Tap (or clap) the rhythms below. Then play and transpose to the keys given.

Pea-nut but-ter, pea-nut but-ter, pea-nut but-ter sand - wich.

1. *mf*

Count: **1** e + a **2** e + a **3** e + a **4** (e) + (a)

- Transpose to **D major** and **A major**.

This rhythm ♩♫ should have the same *feel* as: ♩ ♫

Fudge   sun-dae, fudge sun-dae, fudge sun-dae, fudge.

2. *mf*

Count: **1** (e) + a **2** (e) + a **3** (e) + a **4** (e + a)

- Transpose to **G major** and **D major**.

This rhythm ♫♩ should have the same *feel* as: ♫ ♩

Bub-ble gum, bub-ble gum, bub-ble gum, bub-ble gum.

3. *mf*

Count: **1** e + (a) **2** e + (a) **3** e + (a) **4** e + (a)

- Transpose to **D major** and **A major**.

DISCOVERY

How many 16th notes equal *one* 8th note? _____

Drummer at the Keyboard

- On the closed keyboard lid, tap your R.H. and L.H. together as you count aloud. Can you tap with the metronome at ♩ = **69**?

a. R.H. L.H.

b. R.H. L.H.

- Practice this rhythm puzzle as written.
- Then **transpose** to the keys suggested.

Rhythm Puzzle

Key of _____ Major/Minor

Lively, with precise rhythm (♩ = 72-88)

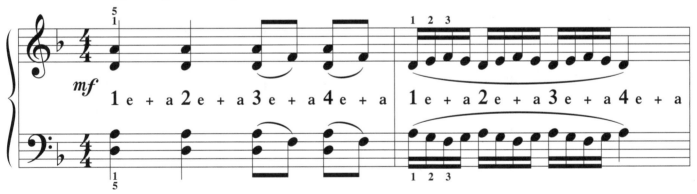

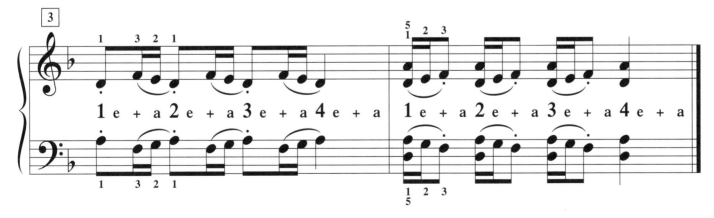

- Transpose to **A minor** and **E minor**. (Remember the F♯ in E minor.)

🖉Theory pp.26-27   ✎Tech p.34   👓Sight pp.76-79

This piece has two tempi (speeds).

- Play the *Adagio* very slowly with big tone.
- Contrast with the *Allegro* using light, fast fingerwork.

Adagio and Allegro

J.C. Bach and F.P. Ricci
(1735–1782) and (1732–1817)
original form

Adagio (very slow) (♩ = 69-76)

Allegro, as in a cadenza (♩ = 104-116)

Remember, a **cadenza** is a showy passage played freely, often without bar lines.

*The lower notes of the L.H. octaves are embellishments from the original single notes.

✏️Theory pp.28-29   🎵Tech p.35   Perf pp.24-25   Sight pp.80-85   FF118

Poco a poco means "little by little."
The term *cresc. poco a poco* means to get louder little by little.

*A mordent is a Baroque ornament that embellishes the principal note by "trilling" with its lower neighbor.

The **character** of a piece refers to the mood of the music.

Like *Adagio and Allegro,* this piece has two contrasting sections, each with its own character and tempo.

Fantasia Con Spirito

Key of ____ Major/Minor

Slowly, with drama (♩ = 100-108)

N. Faber

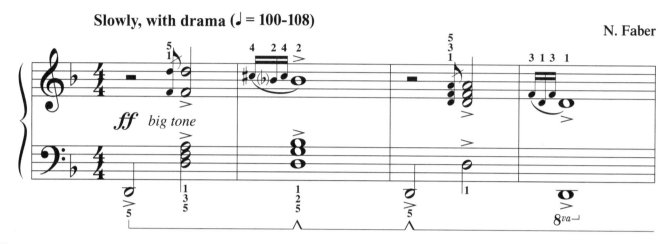

Quickly, mischievously (♩ = 112)

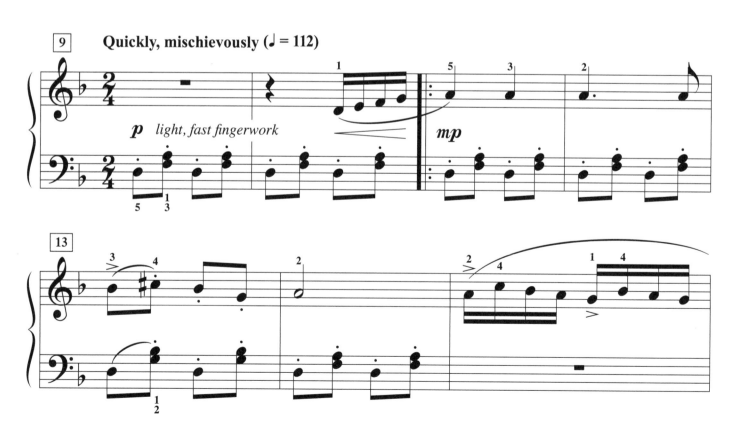

🖉 Theory pp.30-31   ✎ Tech pp.36-37   🎵 Perf pp.26-29   👓 Sight pp.86-89

FF118

molto means "very." Make a
big ritardando for *molto rit.*

D.C. al Fine

molto rit.

A Closer Look at Harmony

- Play these chords built on the C scale.
  Notice that the I, IV, and V chords are **major**. The ii, iii, and vi chords are **minor**.

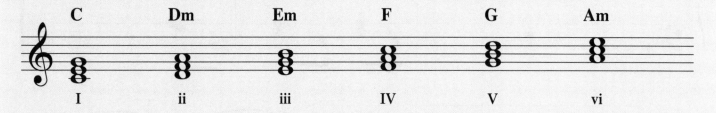

C   Dm   Em   F   G   Am

I   ii   iii   IV   V   vi

- The Pachelbel Canon is based on a repeating 4-measure chord pattern:

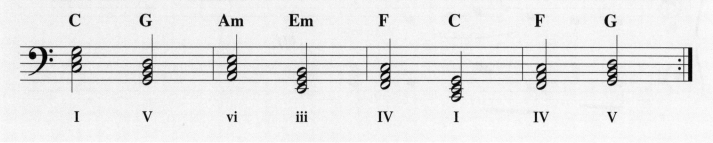

C   G   Am   Em   F   C   F   G

I   V   vi   iii   IV   I   IV   V

- Name the inversions used
  for the R.H. in *measures 1–4*.

Pachelbel Canon

Johann Pachelbel
(1653–1706, Germany)
arranged

Andante (♩ = 100)

chord names: C   G   Am   Em

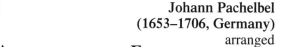
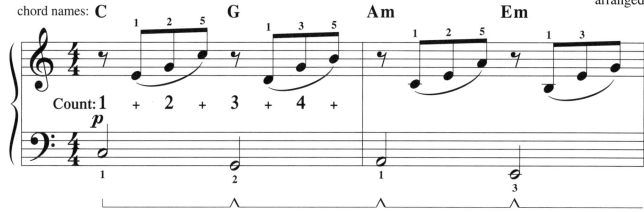

Count: 1   +   2   +   3   +   4   +

p

3   F   C   F   G   C   G

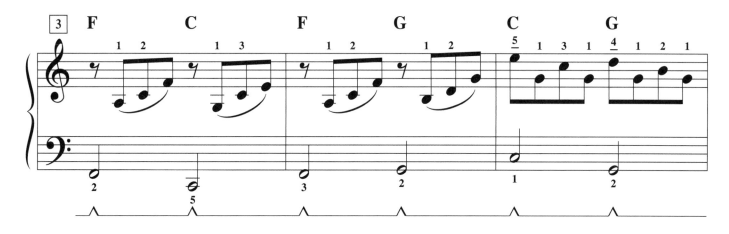

🖉Theory p.32   ✎Tech pp.38-39   🎵Perf pp.30-32   👓Sight pp.90-95

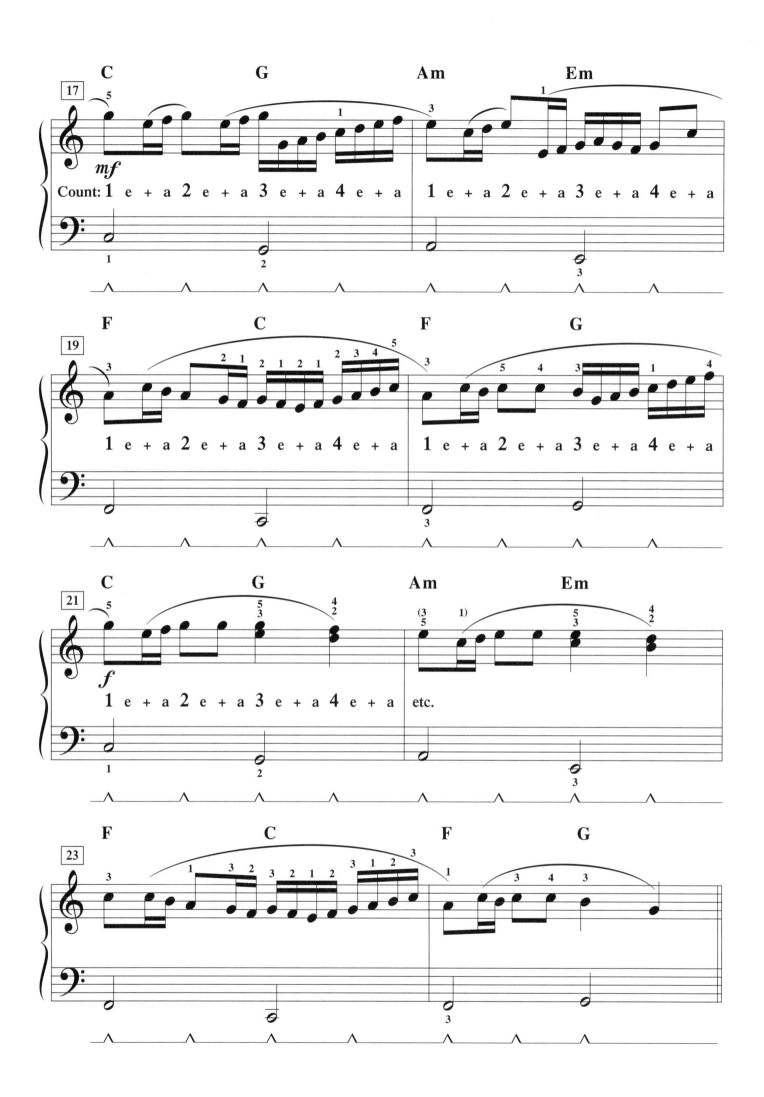

DISCOVERY

Can you play the L.H. bass line for *measures 1–4* by memory?

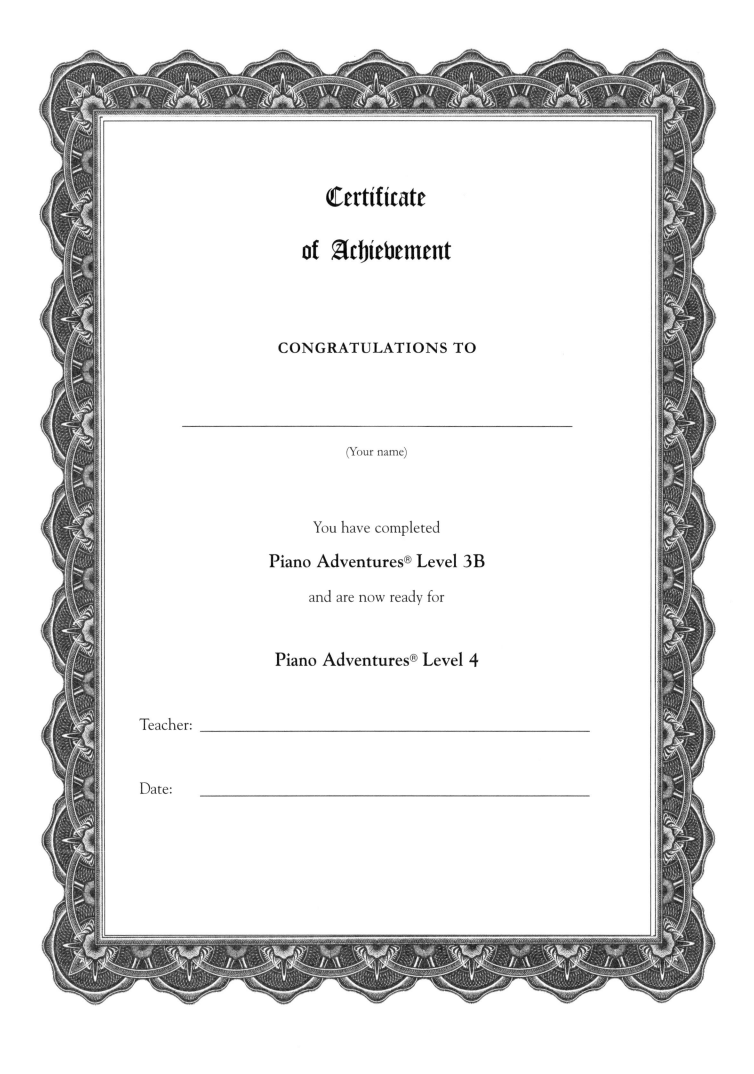

Certificate
of Achievement

CONGRATULATIONS TO

_____

(Your name)

You have completed

Piano Adventures® Level 3B

and are now ready for

Piano Adventures® Level 4

Teacher: _____

Date: _____

FUCK OFF,

I'M DOING DOT-TO-DOT

50 Ridiculous and Hilarious
Dot-to-Dot Creations

DARE YOU

STAMP CO.